*A Time to Live
and a Time to Die*

A Time to Live and a Time to Die

Ronald E. Hignite

RESOURCE *Publications* • Eugene, Oregon

A TIME TO LIVE AND A TIME TO DIE

Copyright © 2013 Ronald Hignite. All rights reserved. Except for brief quotations in critical publications or reviews, no part of this book may be reproduced in any manner without prior written permission from the publisher. Write: Permissions, Wipf and Stock Publishers, 199 W. 8th Ave., Suite 3, Eugene, OR 97401.

Resource Publications
An Imprint of Wipf and Stock Publishers
199 W. 8th Ave., Suite 3
Eugene, OR 97401
www.wipfandstock.com

ISBN 13: 978-1-62564-147-2

Manufactured in the U.S.A.

No part of this book may be reproduced, stored in a retrieval system, or transmitted by any means without the written permission of the author.

The Scripture quotations contained herein are from the King James Version of the Bible.

In loving memory of Len and Carol Hignite,
my Christian father and mother

Contents

Foreword ix
Preface xi

Introduction to *A Time to Live and a Time to Die* 1

A Time to Be Born and a Time to Die 2

A Time to Plant and a Time to Pluck Up That Which Is Planted 5

A Time to Kill and a Time to Heal 6

A Time to Break Down and a Time to Build Up 9

A Time to Weep and a Time to Laugh 10

A Time to Mourn and a Time to Dance 13

A Time to Cast Away Stones and a Time to Gather Stones Together 14

A Time to Embrace and a Time to Refrain From Embracing 17

A Time to Get and a Time to Lose 18

A Time to Keep and a Time to Cast Away 21

A Time to Rend and a Time to Sew 22

A Time to Keep Silence and a Time to Speak 25

A Time to Love and a Time to Hate 26

A Time of War and a Time of Peace 29

Closing to *A Time to Live and a Time to Die* 30

Foreword

RONALD E. HIGNITE DEMONSTRATES in *A Time to Live and a Time to Die* his poetic skills and gives greater understanding and meaning to God's seasons for man as revealed by Solomon in the book of Ecclesiastes. Readers will be inspired by the manner in which he presents the contrasts of the ever-changing seasons of man in poetry and rhyme.

Pastor Gene Williams
Greenville, North Carolina

Preface

It was my pleasure writing *A Time to Live and a Time to Die*. I was inspired to write this book following the personal satisfaction I received in composing my previous books, *The Beatitudes in Poems* and *The Ten Commandments in Poems*. The book contains sixteen poems with fourteen poems covering the twenty-eight seasons in the Bible along with an introductory and closing poem. Each poem is accompanied by a picture that represents one of the seasons expressed in the poem. *The Matthew Henry Commentary* was used as a resource for the interpretation of Scripture.

God's seasons for man were proclaimed by Solomon around 931 BC in the Bible in Ecclesiastes 3:2-8. He revealed in Ecclesiastes 3:1 that for everything there was a season and a purpose. Through these seasons inequities in life are shown, but at the same time harmony and purpose are shown. Things are continually changing, and although man is bound by time, God is not. Instead, God is the master of time. Man must work through these seasons doing the best good he can do. His goal for his efforts is to advance to his final season in the eternal kingdom of God. I hope these poems will be a blessing to its readers.

ECCLESIASTES 3

of all my labour.
on all the works
wrought, and on
d laboured to do:
vanity and vexa-
ere was no profit

myself to behold
ss, and folly: for
hat cometh after
which hath been

t wisdom excell-
t excelleth dark-

eyes *are* in his
alketh in dark-
ceived also that
to them all.
ny heart, As it
so it happeneth
vas I then more
my heart, that

emembrance of
he fool for ever;
is in the days
forgotten. And
n? as the fool.
d life; because
t under the sun
or all *is* vanity

y labour which
sun: because I
man that shall

h whether he
fool? yet shall
labour where-
herein I have

man, *than* that he should
drink, and *that* he should
soul enjoy good in his labour.
I saw, that it *was* from the
God.

25 For who can eat, or who
hasten *hereunto*, more than I?

26 For God giveth to a man
good in his sight wisdom, and
edge, and joy: but to the sinner
giveth travail, to gather and
up, that he may give to him
good before God. This also is
and vexation of spirit.

CHAPTER 3

TO every *thing there is* a season,
a time to every purpose under
heaven:

2 A time to be born, and a time to
die; a time to plant, and a time to
pluck up *that which is* planted;

3 A time to kill, and a time to heal;
a time to break down, and a time to
build up;

4 A time to weep, and a time to
laugh; a time to mourn, and a time to
dance;

5 A time to cast away stones, and a
time to gather stones together; a time
to embrace, and a time to refrain from
embracing;

6 A time to get, and a time to lose;
a time to keep, and a time to cast
away;

7 A time to rend, and a time to sew;
a time to keep silence, and a time to
speak;

8 A time to love, and a time to hate;
a time of war, and a time of peace.

9 What profit hath he that worketh

Introduction to *A Time to Live and a Time to Die*

To everything there is a season,
And each will have its turn,
And every season has a purpose
As each of us will learn.

Day turns into night,
And night turns into day
Just like summer turns into winter,
And then summer comes back into play.

Man's conditions vary
As the seasons flow along,
And God has made these seasons
That for man continue on.

A Time to Be Born and a Time to Die

Ecclesiastes 3:2

There's a time to be born and a time to die,
And in them man has no power
For only God alone will know
When he will set the hour.

What we do while we are here
Each of us must choose,
But we need to use time wisely
Before this time we lose.

For his pleasure God has made us,
And he wants to see the good.
So let's live our lives while here
In the way that we all should.

A Time to Plant and a Time to Pluck Up That Which Is Planted

Ecclesiastes 3:2

There's a time to plant
And a time to pluck up what we sow,
And man is truly blessed
When his crops so richly grow.

These seasons have been given
With great purpose for all mankind.
They are there to help us,
And from them much pleasure we will find.

God has granted us these times
To plant and harvest, too.
We should all be thankful
Since they nourish me and you.

A Time to Kill and a Time to Heal

Ecclesiastes 3:3

There's a time to kill and a time to heal,
And this from God we know
For God will destroy sinful peoples
As he did so long ago.

We should not kill our fellowman,
But at times we have the right
To protect ourselves and others
From those adversaries who show their might.

Then when the killing's over,
Healing must begin
For God desires us all
To live with love and peace within.

A Time to Break Down and a Time to Build Up

Ecclesiastes 3:3

There's a time to break down and a time to build up
Which occur in war and peace.
In war there is destruction.
Then countries build back when battles cease.

In peace strong storms will rage
And tear the land apart,
But man will then build back
Though sometimes will a heavy heart.

Even in our lives,
Breakdowns come within,
But through our faith in God,
We can build up our strength again.

A Time to Weep and a Time to Laugh

Ecclesiastes 3:4

There's a time to weep and a time to laugh,
And these threads run through our life.
We laugh when we are happy,
And we weep when we have strife.

It may be that a loved one's lost
Or a job loss that makes it tough,
Or it may be that we lose at something
When our best is not enough.

Let's be thankful for the good times
That come among the bad,
And be glad when we can laugh
Instead of being sad.

A Time to Mourn
and a Time to Dance

Ecclesiastes 3:4

There's a time to mourn and a time to dance,
And both of these we'll see.
The times for each will vary,
But they'll come for you and me.

When we lose a loved one,
We'll mourn but not alone
For if we seek God's comfort,
He'll not leave us on our own.

Then when things are going well,
In those times we'll dance and smile,
And enjoy that joyous spirit
That pervades us for awhile.

A Time to Cast Away Stones and A Time to Gather Stones Together

Ecclesiastes 3:5

There's a time to cast away stones,
And a time to gather them, too.
If there are things that cause us problems,
They must be removed from me and you.

If stones should cover a field,
And cause the crops not to grow,
Those stones must be cast away
Or the yields from the fields will be low.

Then there will come the time
When stones a man will take.
He'll gather them together,
And with them great structures make.

A Time to Embrace and a Time to Refrain From Embracing

Ecclesiastes 3:5

There's a time to embrace and a time to not embrace
As each of us will learn.
We must be vigilant with people
And one's qualities we must discern.

There are those who are faithful,
And there are those who we trust.
Those persons we can embrace,
But having these traits is a must.

Then there are persons in this life
Who are bad for you and me.
They are disloyal in their manner,
And their embracing should never be.

A Time to Get and a Time to Lose

Ecclesiastes 3:6

There's a time to get and a time to lose,
And we must decide within.
Will we live a life that's good
Or live a life of sin?

God desires we seek the good,
And be the best that we can be.
He desires we seek his truth
So his kingdom one day we'll see.

When sinful ways entrap us,
Then it's time for us to lose
For we must give up what hurts us
And be careful the life we choose.

Bank Savings Account
For John C. Smith

Atlantic National Bank

A Time to Keep and a Time to Cast Away

Ecclesiastes 3:6

There's a time to keep and a time to cast away
As all of us will find
Since possessions for a time are useful,
But then will come a different mind.

What we gain in this life is important,
And we need to protect it the best that we can
For there's a need to establish security
In the life that is lived here by man.

Then the time comes along for us all
When that which we have will mean less,
And if we'll give to the poor and the needy,
We'll find in this life God will bless.

A Time to Rend and a Time to Sew

Ecclesiastes 3:7

There's a time to rend and a time to sew
As in the Bible we have read.
Jacob rent his clothes and mourned
When he found his son was dead.

We all will face the time
When mourning comes along,
And the time for mourning varies,
But for some continues on.

The time will also come
For our broken hearts to mend,
And we can move on with God's help
If on him we will depend.

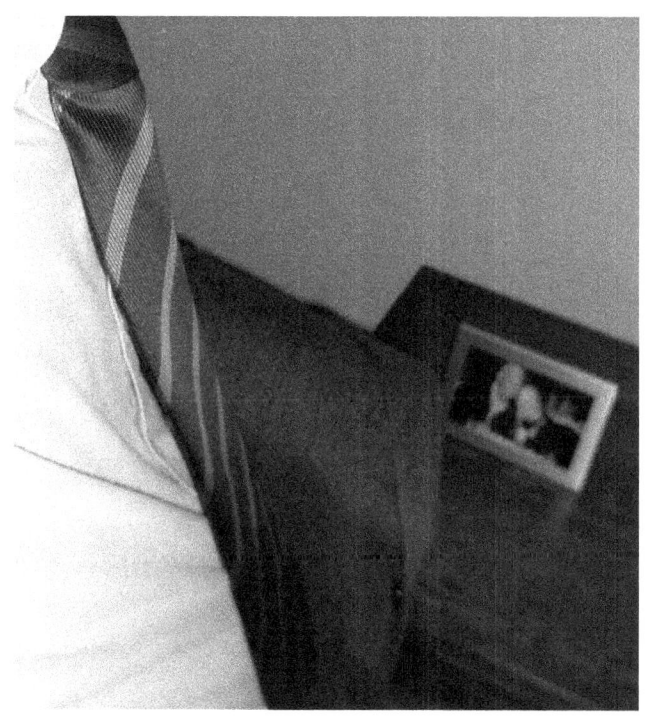

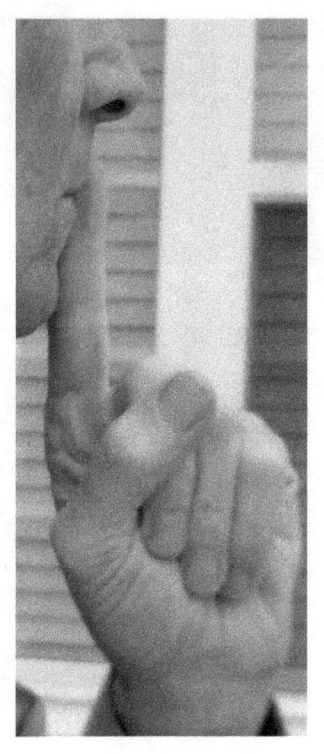

A Time to Keep Silence and a Time to Speak

Ecclesiastes 3:7

There's a time to keep silence and a time to speak,
And each one has its place.
They both do have their value
And both of them we'll face.

When speaking may cause anger,
That's a time we should not speak
For there are those who agitate,
And a confrontation they will seek.

Then the time will come along
When speaking should come about.
It may be in meditation
Or when we stand up for something and must speak out.

A Time to Love and a Time to Hate

Ecclesiastes 3:8

There's a time to love and a time to hate,
And both extremes will see.
One can bring us joy
And the other adversity.

We can love that which is good,
Especially the good traits in men,
But we must avoid the unrighteous,
And stay away from the pitfalls of sin.

The time comes along for us all
When there are things in our life we must hate.
For those things that are sinful and bad,
We must lose swiftly before it's too late.

A Time of War and a Time of Peace

Ecclesiastes 3:8

There's a time of war and a time of peace,
And each will come and go.
As long as there is evil,
Both war and peace we'll know.

We must defend our freedom,
And we must stop others' tyranny.
Therefore wars can't be avoided
Since we must protect one's liberty.

Then when the fighting's over,
That's the time for war to cease,
And a time to achieve a unity,
And create an enduring peace.

Closing to *A Time to Live and a Time to Die*

To everything there is a season
As we've learned along the way,
And to every season there is a purpose
Like when the sun gives light to day.

These seasons may cause us problems
For the limitations they impose on man,
But these seasons show harmony and purpose
And are parts of God's master plan.

God has made all things beautiful
Whether it be insect or flower,
And everything's been made in its time
Through his artistic design and his power.

www.ingramcontent.com/pod-product-compliance
Lightning Source LLC
Chambersburg PA
CBHW070750050426
42449CB00010B/2403